BELLA

My name is Bella. I am what the humans call a Border collie. How clever those humans are, they can figure out where a dog originates from but we, dogs, know that we all descend from that wild and mystical creature called the wolf. The name "Border Collie" comes from the fact that, a long time ago, my ancestors lived in a place near a border between two countries called England and Scotland. Mankind, always ready to put to use any animal and replace them to do the work they do not want or cannot do themselves, decided that we would be good for keeping sheep. I mean, that's a bit silly considering that even now, sheep is the favourite meal of our ancestor the wolf. So I reckon we must have kept embedded in our genes the famous stance we have when we look after those not terribly bright animals, crawling low to direct them where we want them to go, a long time ago the direction being straight into a pack of wolves teeth !

Myself, I can't stand sheep. We often go to the mountains in the summer and there are flocks of them everywhere. I must admit that the border collies who work there, running after hundreds of sheep do an amazing job keeping control of those unruly animals. It is an absolute wonderful sight to see two dogs going non-stop over long distances all in order to keep the pack of sheep as one.

However personally I find them not very clean and a bit simple minded and much prefer to live my carefree and happy life, a dog's life, doing not very much. My human pack, Bill and Chris, see to that. I must admit that as a pack, they are quite unique and look after me superbly. Long walks, meals on time, a bowl of water always full, a good bed to sleep on, not much else a dog could desire.

In my humble and doggy way, I shall endeavour to explain further where the relationship between human and dog sometimes goes amiss and fails to meet what is needed for everyone to be relaxed living with each other. After all, I have heard it said that dog is the human closest friend and it would be best if we could work together for a better understanding of each other's needs. This way everyone would be happy.

BILL

So you want a dog? Not an easy decision and one which needs to be taken with great care. It is such a responsibility to take care of another creature, one which will put all its trust in you and to look after it properly. Mankind have taken it upon them to make dogs their most common animal friend, apart from that other great predator the cat. So acquiring a friendly dog ready to love humans, has to be carefully thought of. What is the point of making your new companion miserable?

There are so many things to consider when you wish to acquire a dog. Where do you live, in an apartment or a big country house, are you at home all day or away at work? Do you have children; do you want an animal for company for yourself? Can you spare the time to look after your dog, not to simply ignore your four legged companion after the novelty has worn off. Can you afford to feed it, after all a few scraps are ok with a dog but they do need a basic substantial meal once a day? For that meal you give your four legged friend, it will be humbly thankful.

Of course all the above points need to be considered carefully before you take the step of acquiring your dog. You must also think what race is suited for you and your family. Living in a small apartment and acquiring a huge dog is running straight into disaster. Again if you are at work all day, forget the large size dog, in fact best to forget acquiring a dog at all. Dogs are essentially creatures of the wild and need space and the feeling of freedom. To be cooped up between four walls all day is not right for this animal, whether your new chosen companion is large or small. And that would be when the relationship starts to deteriorate. Can you take your dog with you if you go away or can it be looked after by someone else? And please be careful with the "pet hotels" where a dog is cooped up for hours in a very small enclosure with a simple cement floor serving as grass. Dogs have some feelings about how and where they live and although they don't need much comfort, a minimum of it is good.

You also will need to think who you will acquire your dog from. It could be from a breeder, but again you must check carefully how the puppies were bred and if the breeder has a good reputation. Unfortunately there have been some horror stories about this. It could be from someone you know or from one of the many dogs refuges where the humans who work there look after the abandoned dogs with so much heart and kindness and try to restore in those sad animals faith into mankind and that not all humans are cruel and mean. I could name for example a lady who works voluntarily at such a refuge. She also comes and helps in all sorts of way at the canine club where I now train with Bella. Her dedication to those abandoned pets is an example to all, and although she appears to be a very strong person mentally, she seems to have tears in her eyes when she talks about some of the animals she has had to care for at the refuge, almost unable to describe the sad creatures she has to deal with.

"A dog is for life", one of the famous and so true sentence used by a well-known animals refuge centre. When we go to the canine school with Bella where we train for Agility, we have met some of those "saved" dogs and I can tell you, they don't appear in their demeanour to have a pretty story to tell. But most of them are happy now and give a hundred times back the kindness which their new human companions show them.

So don't forget, if you want a dog you must be prepared to love it.

Before anything else all a dog needs is love.

BELLA

I was born seven years ago. My dad is called Chico. He is what the humans call a peasant, without pedigree, a low born. But what he may lack in good lineage, he certainly makes up in stance and character. A good solid specimen of a dog, healthy, good muscles, not the thin looking Border collie you see nowadays, bred for speed on the competition courses. He is the kind of dog who seems to say, "look I can take care of myself so don't mess with me"!

I have heard Bill and Chris say that, although I am a female dog, I look like my Dad. I am certainly not the dainty kind, I would call myself athletic looking, good strong legs and back, shiny fur and bright eyes. I have also heard it said that I also look very clever! In fact when I do something funny or unusual, Chris always says to me "What a clever girl", so it must be true as I have all faith in her.

Well the intelligence I believe I owe to my mum, Samba. Now here is a real lady, she has titles and long pedigree names, a kind of dog princess. She is soft and loving and although I prefer when I see my parents to play with my dad who knows how do give a good rough play fight, I also adore being with my mum who gives me lots of licks and kisses.

I was born in a litter of seven puppies. The human pack where my mum and dad live speak a different language from Chris and Bill and I believe from a tender age I could already understand three different human languages. Not many human babies can boast about the same ability in languages at that age!

But one day came the sad day to eventually become the happy days when I was to leave my brothers and sisters and my mum and dad. That is what the humans had decided. I had already an idea that it would happen to me as already three of my brothers had disappeared after visits from various humans. My mum, trying to reassure what was left of her litter, kept on licking us and cuddling us, but the famous day came for me. Bill and Chris arrived!

What a good day that was. Chris came to me, so much love showing in her eyes, I had no doubt she was the one. I climbed in her arms, she cuddled me and the fate of my future life was sealed.

We went on a long journey to what was to become my second home. On the way, I was as sick as a dog! Fright I suppose, my first exposure to motorcars. To this day, I still hate travelling in those beastly noisy round wheels monsters taking you at such speed to unknown destination. When in one I never feel I am in charge of my destiny and can only lay there, shaken and frightened waiting for the journey to end. But being brave and knowing that Bill and Chris are there eases matters somewhat.

I must admit I had a royal welcome. Special bedding, special bowls, special food, a real queen's surroundings.

However things started to turn sour with the toilet training. When I was with my mum and dad, I could do whatever nature ordered whenever and wherever I wanted. We were in an enclosure in a garden and used to roam fairly free and there did not seem to be any rules about where and when to do what I needed to do. But the rules suddenly became different!

I started going back to my old accustomed way and Bill decided to take matters into his own hand.

Somehow I had broken one of the basic rule, I had wetted the floor in the lounge where my bed was installed and deposited a nice healthy pooh nearby. It was the middle of the winter but Bill was pitiless and having lifted me from the warm house, deposited me in that cold and wet stuff called snow. I mean, how unkind! I just didn't know what was happening, especially when Bill started murmuring strange words like pee and pooh.

Whether it was the fact that I was definitely not keen on going to do what was intended in the cold garden or whether I couldn't be bothered, I do not remember. But I finally got the message after being taken bodily from the house into the garden and made to stay there until I did what was expected of me. Not being a masochist by nature, I quickly got the message and saw that if I was going to live in peace and harmony with Bill and Chris I would need to use their toilet methods and humour them! But I ask you, do humans have that kind of behaviour with their own babies? There would be a real human outcry if any parents were to use the same behaviour about potty training. I believe that human's babies are lucky in that respect, parents put a kind of cloth around their baby's bellies and they can produce whatever nature intended whenever they please. And get cleaned up afterwards!! Personally I think I would look rather stupid going about my business with one of that cloth around my waist, but I am now fully house trained as humans call it and know that it is the grass I should grace my toilet needs with not the Persian carpet. I tell you, where is the difference?

However, please under no circumstances revert to those barbaric methods I have heard some of my chum dogs speak about. These vary from having your nose rubbed in whatever you deposited, or worse being smacked, kicked, told that you are a dumb dog, and other best forgotten cruel methods. It just does not work with a poor puppy dog who really would not know what is happening to him, especially if the punishment is dished out quite a while after the so called crime has been committed. Remember that although dogs are terribly clever, they do not have the same comprehension of time as humans, and punishing a puppy for the unmentionable, i.e. wetting the floor, hours after the act has been committed, is not only cruel, it would serve no purpose, the puppy not knowing why it was suddenly being physically abused.

BILL

- From the first day you acquire your puppy take him out at regular hours and always to the same spot outside, preferably grass. The puppy will associate going out and that particular spot with toilet time.

- If you have to go out and leave your puppy for a while, take him outdoors as soon as you get back.

- When the puppy produces whatever you want him to produce, give him a reward, speak to the puppy nicely, words like "good girl, good boy". The puppy will know that it has done something terribly clever and will be keen to renew the experience especially if there is a reward at the end of it.

- Don't forget that when puppies are young and still with their siblings, the mother will clean her babies. As you are not presumably prepared to do the same, at least do your utmost and give him a chance to learn by himself what is required to live in harmony within your family.

- Best of all, try to train your puppy to do his toilet on command. It will serve its purpose if one day you decide to enter the arena of competitions. If your dog soils the competition area it will be an instant elimination from that competition.

BELLA

I am the most obedient dog in the world. So I have heard Bill say! It is not difficult really, simple rules and understanding which if you, as a dog, do not rebel to, make life between humans and dogs so much easier.

We are as a result of living with humans, exposed to the human world and its danger. No good having a crazy animal rushing around aimlessly in the streets, the consequences would be disastrous.

The same applies when dogs are confronted to other humans. The other humans do not always know how to react and that can send all sorts of negative messages to a dog's brain. The fact that a dog is obedient and will behave to its human owner's commands will avoid possible dangerous situations.

I was introduced to obedience classes by Bill and Chris because I must say, as a puppy, I was pretty unruly. All I wanted was to run free in the fields, we lived at that time in a wonderful farm with endless space and to boot it all with a small river. Such fun it was to speed along, jump over the grass, hide in the bushes, throw myself in the water, I was a complete maniac, in the nicest possible way of course, as Bill and Chris kept on laughing at my crazy ways of romping about.

So the big decision was taken, I was to become a scholar! Well I already knew three different languages, so I thought I was above all that, but there was no escape. Bill decided that someone would come to our house to give me the rudiments of good dog behaviour. I ask you, what for, much more fun to just run wild and without a care in the world!

The famous day arrived for lesson one. My teacher was a female human and seemed at first very friendly and kind. She put me through all sorts of commands, sit, lay down, stand up. Ok, at first I did not know those words but as she kept on prodding me and pushing me until she got the right movement and at the end of it I was given a nice titbit, I thought I would humour her and do as she wanted.

So the first few lessons went well, especially as I was able to put into use my newly acquired skills and respond to Bill's commands when we went on long walks afterwards. He was really pleased and as he was pleased, so was I. Dogs only want that kind of relationship, a happy owner means a happy dog.

Things started to deteriorate with my school teacher when she decided it was time to make me walk in a more sedate way and to stop me bouncing about like some deranged frog. I have personally nothing against frogs but they do have a weird way of going about. This was the moment of truth, the big challenge, I was to be put on a lead.

Well I tell you, at first, the experience was very unpleasant. I just could not stand having this piece of leather around my throat and a long piece of leather restraining me to go where I wanted. There was a lot of pulling on my part and a lot of pulling back on hers. It became a personal war from both parties. But I was not on the winning side as she kept on coming back for more lessons.

However the final crunch came one day when she decided in order to try to stop me being so unruly, to place a different collar around my neck. Some kind of horrible device with bit of sharp metal which if I pulled would choke me and hurt me. Well that was that I decided. I was not going to comply with these savages' ways of trying to teach a dog to walk calmly. I was anything but calm, I was very angry.

I decided the best course of action was to go on strike. I laid down and whatever this teacher tried to encourage me to get up and walk went completely over my head. I was not going to bulge. Luckily for me Bill and Chris were always present when the lessons took place. They stopped all this straight away and Bill put a stop to the lesson. I was to see this person no more. Good riddance, I had won the battle, but not the war!

Bill decided to carry on with the obedience training himself. He made us join a canine club where unruly puppies like me are given the rudiments of good behaviour. A kind of private schooling for dogs, with proper teachers! You could call it a military academy for dogs!

That was great fun as I also suddenly found out that I was not on my own in the world as a dog, there were so many others, all shapes and sizes and most of them so friendly. What happy times I had when after the lessons, all the puppies were let free and we were running after each other, ear biting in a mock play fight, laying in the grass together, rolling in it, and basically having a whale of a time.

I stayed at the school for six months and after that time I was the perfect scholar. Whatever commands Bill gave me were instantly obeyed and he was so pleased with me. He was the perfect teacher to have, always a kind word, a pat on the head, a tasty reward in his hand if I did particularly well at something.

The big day came when we had, both of us, to pass a test, a kind of final examination to see if I could join the "good behaviour" dog pack. Well I was not going to let Bill down, I could feel deep down that he was nervous. We both performed excellently and I heard Bill say to Chris afterwards that we had both received maximum points for the exam. Whatever that meant, it made Bill happy and therefore I was happy.

I had progressed from being a wild crazy puppy and was now a fully trained dog, acting responsibly and sensibly and most of all reacting positively to what Bill wanted me to do. But I must say that I would not have been able to achieve this without his patience, kindness and understanding of how to treat a dog.

After all, we have feelings too and all we dogs need is love!

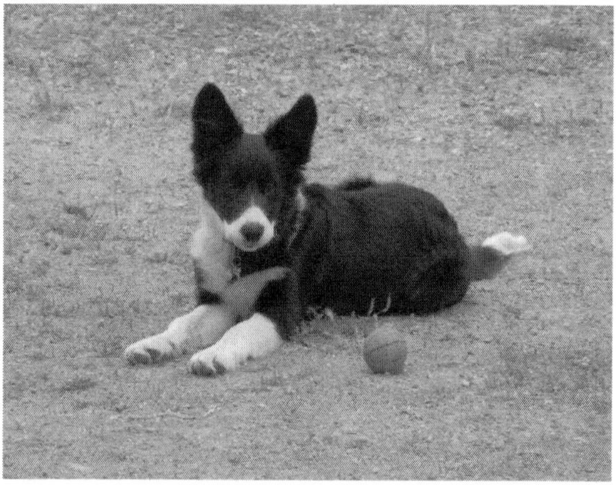

BILL

Now that you have trained your puppy to be clean within the house, then there is the further challenge of trying to make it do what YOU want on YOUR command. It is easily forgotten when you look at your adorable furry and soft eyes animal that it is primarily a wild animal, with a mind of its own! Asking your dog to obey your orders is vital for its own safety but also for your own peace of mind.

Let's talk about the training for making your dog walk to your heel with a lead. You will be immediately confronted when putting a collar and lead on a dog with a bewildered animal who thinks it is being punished for some unknown reason. After all dogs like to run free and wherever they want, their understanding of walking by your side in a sedate manner is, to say the least, nil to start with.

As in all manners of training your dog, the essential and prime thing is to obtain its trust.

Once a lead has been put on a puppy its first and prime reaction will be to pull, trying to get away from this restricting object. Why do they pull, well this is easy to analyse. They want freedom, they may want to be in front to either see if the road ahead is without danger but mostly it will want to run around and sniff about.

In order to stop your puppy pulling on his lead, you should first of all stop yourself pulling on the lead. If your animal pulls one way and you the other, it will soon be a battle of mind over matter and become a war between the two of you. Instead when your dog pulls simply stop then start walking again. Each time the dog stops with you give him a treat and a huge comforting pat.

You can also try to stop and stand in front of your dog. He will be unable to see where he is going or what is in front of him and will automatically stop himself. When this happens, again a treat and a pat are called for.

Another method is to for you to stop and turn your back on your dog. He will be curious and come and see what you are up to, whether this could be some kind of new game. The mere fact that your puppy stopped deserve a reward and a pat.

Of course if you attend Obedience Classes in a Canine Club, and I firmly recommend that you do, there will be all kinds of different methods to teach the above. Nothing in this kind of training is black and white, so listen and take in any advice that different instructors may give you. But most of all and I will repeat myself try and achieve any training with love and patience and most of all without any corporal punishments. Eventually your dog will understand what you expect from him and will happily walk in a sedate and calm manner by your side.

BELLA

Relationship between humans and dogs. Now, that's a huge challenge. For my part, I consider myself lucky. My human pack, Bill and Chris, does not seem to have any hang ups about who is the boss so no one takes advantage of the situation. Mutual respect I call it.

For some very peculiar reason, humans seem to think that they have to be dominant over dogs. Why? Ok, we may not be as clever as humans on a number of things, inventing all these wonderful little gadgets that the humans do not seem to be without. But on the other hand I think that we dogs are pretty bright too.

We can do all sorts of things that humans cannot do, we can hear better, our sense of smell is far superior, we can run faster, we can see in the dark and most of all we don't mind working for humans or helping them in any way. You would hardly expect the opposite!

The working dog, now that's a pretty wonderful animal. Think of all the humans who have been saved one way or another by dogs. The wonderful and strong St Bernard who looks for people lost in the snow. They usually search in a pack of three and when they find the person buried in the snow, one of them stays with the person to keep that person warm and the other two run to fetch help.

The Malinois or German Shepherd dogs who find people buried during earthquakes, relentlessly sniffing for the smallest of smell which might indicate a person below rubble. Hours of patient training and understanding between the dog and its trainer have gone into this particular wonderful partnership.

Soldiers injured during the wars, found by some four legged friend who will run to find another human in order to help the injured person. Some dogs were used during the two last world wars to carry messages to different fighting units, ignoring the danger of flying bullets or an intended shot from the enemy. Some dogs were actually awarded special merit crosses for their achievements during the war.

The Labradors, German Shepherds, Border Collies who

help blind people by becoming their eyes. It is wonderful to see those gentle creatures walking slowly with their owners, ensuring that they will come to no harm whilst moving from one place to another.

The dogs that are taken to hospitals to comfort sick children and elderly people. The sudden spark of happiness in those dull eyes, ravaged by pain and endless hours of stillness.

In Africa, the local dogs defend the herd of cows, whether they are in the open grazing with usually only a couple of children to look after things or when they are taken in the village compound at night. Those dogs will fearlessly attack any wild animal including lions to defend the treasured and valued possessions of their owners, the herds of cattle.

The list of how, we, dosg can help the humans is endless. We have the physical ability to put ourselves to the service of mankind, and all this without expecting anything in return that a pat on the head and a kind word. We do it with love and for love.

So why do some humans treat us dogs as some kind of subspecies, only good enough to be kicked, shouted at (please why shout? we definitely are not deaf !), thrown a bone if we are lucky, left to sleep out in all weather, chained to a wall days after days. WHY? Does this make humans feel dominant? Personally I call it cruelty and stupidity.

I have already mentioned that the club where I go to school with Bill has a few of the most unfortunate fellow dogs in the world. The outcast, the abandoned. I can assure you they don't have a pretty tale to say, and the horror stories are too much to bear.

In my humble doggy way I feel that relationship between humans and dogs should be based on kindness and love. If treated properly and dare I say, humanly, any of my fellow dogs will respond with such love and enthusiasm to any request or command it is given, ready to please and cooperate in whatever task it is asked to perform.

The opposite side of the coin is the manner in which some humans feel that they have to treat their four-legged friend, in the most inhuman way.

Bill and Chris are so caring towards me and in response I am always there for them, protecting them and giving them my absolute uncalculated love. I often hear Bill say when I look at him: look at those eyes, some much love in them. And it's true, I would do anything for both of them.

I spend a lot of time with my human pack, Bill and Chris and listen carefully to their conversation. I mean, you never know when a command may be directed at me and I have to be ready. However, most of the time and if they talk about dogs which seems is one of Bill's favourite subject, they talk about general behaviour. Not of the dogs but of the human attitude towards their companions. I often hear Bill say "To train a dog is not difficult but to train its owner is".

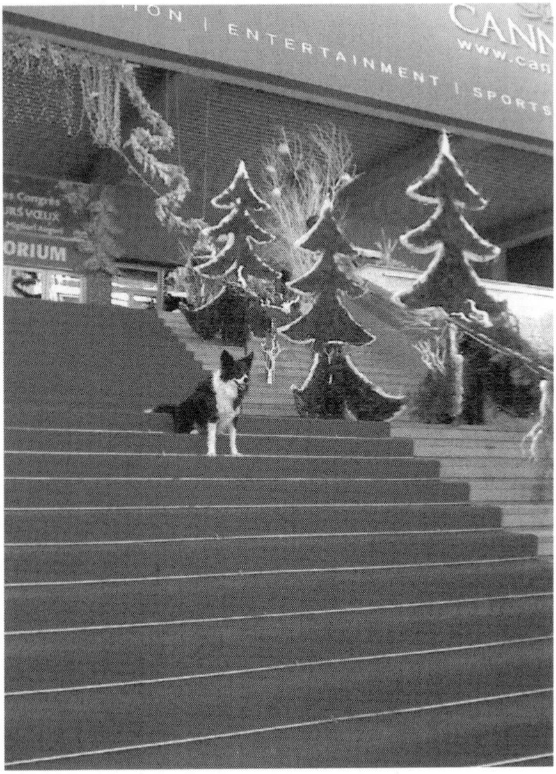
ENTERTAINMENT
SPORTS

BILL

Above anything else and whatever you want to achieve with your four legged companion, avoid corporal punishment. It will serve no purpose. The dog will fear you but will not love you and will only obey your command unwillingly and fearfully, hoping not to get another dose of yells, kicks or other "undoggy" ways. A dog will work for its owner only responding to gentleness, patience, firmness and mostly love. "Make a dog love you and he will never forsake you", a true sentence written by a famous writer experienced with dog's training.

However it is important that a dog obeys to live in harmony in the human world. To answer a call at once and not to ignore it. An owner must do its utmost, whether taking his young puppy to a club to be trained by experts or whether trained by the owner himself. But a dog cannot live happily within the context of a human pack without learning a few behaviour rules.

Look and observe your dog. Some dogs are more sensitive than others and will respond differently in various circumstances. But this could be said of any living creature.

If your dog does something really silly, well anyway silly to you, human, try to understand the reason. I mean, to the dog it may not be silly, there may be and certainly is a reason for this silly behaviour. Analyse why, find a way to correct the mistake once you understand it and put in place with your dog as a partner a solution so that the mistake is not repeated. Gently going over correcting bad behaviour can be painstakingly long in time and it is true that most humans do not seem to find or wish to find the time to devote to train their dog. But it is essential for a harmonious life together. After all, humans try their best to educate their children to their own standards of behaviour, it makes sense that a four legged companion should be trained the same way.

I have often observed some of dogs on walks with their owners. Sometimes there are some really fun situations to be observed. For example, a dog is taken for a walk. Most of the time the poor animal, even in open space, will be on a lead. Why, because the owner does not trust his dog. Does not trust that he will not run away, does not trust that he will come back when called back. Whose fault is that? Well certainly not the dog. Can you imagine the situation, this poor animal is suddenly in the open after probably been cooped up for hours, is left loose without a lead, and just as he is having great fun sniffing all sorts of wonderful and unusual smells, is called back to be tied again. Well the first reaction from the dog will be "I don't want that, I don't want to be tied again, I want to carry on sniffing and I will not come back until I am ready". Quite fun to see the dog running away with the owner running behind calling him by name and getting no response. All of the time the dog will run faster and to him it will become a great game. But inevitably when caught or fed up with the game he will be smacked for being a "bad dog". So positive training with your dog is essential so he can trust you to do the right thing by him. Immediate response from your dog must be achieved with patience and mutual respect.

It is most important that your dog comes back when called. In order to train him it must understand and obey the four essential commands: Sit – Down – Sit Up - Stay. Without those four basics it will be impossible to progress.

To train your dog to come back to you, you first of all put him in a sit, down, stay position. You will then go away from your dog, say to start with two metres. You should then look at your dog (who hopefully will not have moved) and in a firm voice call him to you. As soon as he is there by your side, all happy, don't forget the magical treat and pat. If successful with a five metres distance, then make the distance longer. The big final test is then to hide a short distance from your dog and then having him find you. He will be so happy, thinking this is a great game, and again a reward and lots of "good boy or good girl" are essential.

One important point to be stressed is that you must always tie up your dog if leaving it even for a few seconds outside a shop. If anything attracts its attention and it is not tied, this could lead to a disaster. However obedient you may think your dog is, something can always distract its attention, a cat for example. And you know the relationship between those two animals, most of the times the dog always chases the cat!

BELLA

Today is an exciting day, even more exciting that all the other days. It is going to be my first competition at Agility. I am now nearly two years old, have been training for this sport for over one year and Bill thinks I am ready to enter the arena.

Bill and Chris wake up, it's still dark outside, must be really early. However, I still go and do my rounds of the garden just in case some unwelcomed visitor is lurking in the bushes. All clear and I go to have my breakfast. But nasty surprise, the quantity is half of what I usually get. Not a good start of the day as if there is one thing I enjoy tremendously, it's my meals! Bill laughs and says, well Bella you don't want to go to a competition on a full stomach! Can't see the point but I shall humour him.

Then we are off, still in the dark, car has been packed to the roof with all sorts of things, picnic basket – hope there is something for me, chairs for the humans to sit on, cage for me to rest in and all sorts of needed items.

The journey goes on for ever, still in the dark, novelty of this exciting competition starts to wear off. Finally we arrive. Car is parked and suddenly all I can hear is a cacophony of various barks, it seems there are hundreds of dogs everywhere. What's going on?

Bill takes me out of the car and boy do I need to stretch my legs after that awfully long journey. We go on a little walk and I get the opportunity to say hello to a few friends. Most of those dogs are unknown to me but being very social and polite I say hello anyway.

Some of the dogs have obviously got up on the wrong paw as they growl at me but I shall play my princess act and totally ignore them.

The sun finally appears and puts a light on the famous place where we are going to compete. What a mess! There are humans everywhere mostly accompanied by their four legged friends, some have two or three on a lead, all bumping into each other and wanting to go their own way. What an unruly lot!

Then the competitions start. We are number 16. And suddenly it's our turn to enter the "arena". Bill takes me to the front of the starting obstacle and tells me in a very firm way "Stay, don't move". Well difficult to obey, I am rearing to go and do my thing. But being well conditioned to listen to his orders I do as I am told. Then a flick of his hand encouraging me to come forward and we are off. What fun ...... Over jumps, into tunnels, over bridges, going through the slalom, all this as quick as we can. I could go much faster but can see that Bill is struggling to keep up my pace so being a good friend I slow down, listening to his commands and concentrating on the job to be done. Then it's the final three jumps, Bill encourages me from afar to go over those as fast as I can, and I reach the end of the course. Bill is there, so proud of me, giving me a huge cuddle and best treat of all, my favourite ball to run after. That was fun, I am ready to do it again.

That day, we did three different courses, all with various courses to follow, some more difficult than others.

And the big moment came, the prize giving. Suddenly I see Bill get up, leading me with him to a person who gives him a cup. Can't believe it, we have won a prize, and this on our first competition. Bill is so proud and I must say that I am too. After all both of us were new at that game, had to compete against much more experienced dogs and have done bloody well.

The end of a very perfectly fun day!

BILL

Having acquired this wonderful Border collie and trained her to perfect obedience, I could see her potential of intelligence. She grasped orders so quickly, always ready to respond to commands. When I took her to her first obedience classes at the canine club, I could see straight away that she would need something more stimulating in her life than just those classes. After a few weeks of training at Obedience Classes and doing constantly the same exercises, Bella got so bored that she used to lay down and fall asleep between each exercise! One of the instructors said to me: "why don't you introduce her to Agility classes", she might enjoy it.

Bella took to it like fish to water. She is made for this. Being strong and muscular, she can jump over obstacles with such ease, seeming to fly over them. I have a great photo of her taken during one Agility competition where she is going over a jump and at the same time turning her head towards the photographer seeming to smile at the camera. What a show off!

She was soon ready to enter competitions. The first one was a great success as we received a prize on that occasion. I think Bella knew how proud I was as she was going around with me with her head high and tail to match!

These competitions are very demanding, both on the dogs and the owners. It's a very long and tiring day.

Early morning call, usually around four thirty in the morning, ready to leave the house an hour later. Most competitions are far from one another and most likely at least one hour and a half from home. Chris, being a lazy cat, gets up to prepare food for the day and sees me and Bella off, no doubt going back to bed straight after. Wise lady.

The drive is always a traumatic moment for Bella, don't know if she will ever get used to that way of travelling. She is so stressed after a long journey and I have to use all my patience and persuasion to calm her down. Not a good start for a competition but she is eventually pacified.

On arrival we have to give our details and receive a competitor's number, it's a long wait. I usually take Bella for a little walk about where she can exchange a few social sniffs with her fellow dogs. Some of those dogs are absolutely crazy, pulling and barking at the top of their voices, but Bella just gives them the royal stare and looks at them as though they are completely bonkers.

Then it's time for us two to compete. You are given a chance as a competitor to recognize the course prior to start each competition, without your dog of course. It is a good thing if you are not the first one to go, gives you a chance to observe the good points and bad mistakes made by other competitors. Bella's category is C which is determined by her size. The majority of the opponents are also border collies as these dogs seem to excel at that sport. Some of them are so quick, led by very fast running owners! Difficult for me at my age to adapt to Bella's speed so I now use a competition device whereas I direct from afar and don't run all the obstacles with her, thus saving my breath. Most competitions are over in less than one minute, but it is one minute of intense speed and concentration and both owner and dog are panting like dogs at the end.

When starting the competition I, of cours,e always feel a bit nervous, only normal to have the adrenaline flowing, and I know this feeling transfers to the dog. Luckily Bella is a very calm dog and she goes in front of the first obstacle waiting for my signal as though she hasn't a care in the world, looking around as though saying "what the hell am I doing here" and "stop the noise please".

But she knows that at the end and whatever the result of that particular course, I will be there, giving her a huge hug and a treat. And to her that is the most important reward.

We have been doing those competitions together for nearly six years now. It's quite an involved sport and so interesting to do. The satisfaction to guide your dog on the course with verbal orders and hand movements a good five meters from one another and working in perfect coordination – well most of the times - is tremendously satisfying, for both the human and the dog. It's easy to see how much each dog enjoys the event, barking with happiness, ears up and tail wagging, going at full speed as though their lives depended on it. The happiness at the end of it all! Whether the run was successful or not.....simply the satisfaction of competing together.

Bella has now acquired over those years a very nice collection of cups and prizes. They have a place of honour on shelves in the garage and I take great pride in showing these to any visitor who is interested. Bella of course simply takes it for granted and doesn't bat an eyelid when complimented on these achievements.

However one thing I would wish to mention regarding those Agility competitions is the fact that dogs without a pedigree are not allowed to do some of the courses which take place in all competitions. For example, Bella can enter some competitions for dogs of any birth or race but when it comes to the selective first, second and third degrees competitions so that a dog can be confirmed as being of its true race, Bella cannot enter having no official pedigree.

This therefore penalizes her from entering competitions to be selected for international competitions and represent her country of birth. This seems so unfair. After all if a dog is capable of achieving wonderful results, what is having a pedigree got to do with it. Being born of parents with of the same race does not make a champion but it seems that these criteria are the only ones which select a dog for international competitions. Luckily this does not apply to the world of sport or a great number of tremendous athletes would be left out.

In one of the competitions we recently entered, the winner was a "mongrel", followed by Bella who also has no pedigree registration. Yet those two dogs achieved better times and went through the course without any errors. If they were allowed to be participants in international competitions and represent the country they live in who knows what they would achieve, yet they are refused this opportunity all in the name of keeping the races pure. My true conviction is that one has nothing to do with the other, a dog can be of pure race whether German shepherd or Jack Russell and can be absolutely useless in a competition. Yet some of the ones who have the natural ability are forbidden to these reunions. The whole system is very unfair.

BELLA

I am such a lucky dog, I live in a part of the world where we are surrounded by woods and rivers and the house itself is set in large grounds where I can roam freely.

To me the best time of the day, apart from meal times, is when we all go for a walk. There are so many places to choose from and to run freely in semi wild areas is a real treat for a dog. I feel sorry for some of my poor fellow dogs who only have a small piece of tarmac to investigate on their daily outings, and that is for the lucky ones. Best not to mention the ones who are tied all day and never get the chance to even sniff a blade of grass.

Anyway, I know when it's time for walks. Bill and Chris have a ritual to which I have become conditioned, they always put on the same jackets and shoes and I can smell from these if it is walking time. Usually in the morning I do give my check up on them after shower time, and that is not to see whether they have washed their "paws" properly but simply to determine if its "clothes walking time" when they dress.

We sometime go straight from the house into the woods or sometime take the car. That second option is not so good for me but I put up with it knowing what waits at the end of the journey. Then we are off.

What joy when we arrive, I immediately set off at a good running pace as though I was some kind of demented and wild animal, but it's simply to show how excited I am. Then I slow down a bit and get on with the serious task of sniffing everywhere and investigating all corners, even on the walks I know well. After all and that's not noticed by the humans but so many different kind of animals have passed by and I have to find out which potential enemy has been around.

Sometimes I recognize the smell of my pal down the road, that very self-sufficient rogue of a dog who thinks he is the king's bee and tries to take advantage of my kind and social nature. But I soon put him in his place when he starts being frisky with me and let him know in no uncertain terms that I am a "lady" so no liberties are allowed by me.

Anyway, back to our run, I escalade hills, disappear behind bushes, run at full speed in the fields, and dive into the river if there is one. This is great fun and all that time I know that I am safe as Bill and Chris are never far behind me. I do my bit of guard dog though from time to time and if I smell danger ahead, I come running to them and walk with them until danger has passed. I think they know this, I do it mostly when Chris is on her own with me, after all she is the weak human in the pack and I have to do my bit to protect her.

I do have some scary encounters. There are lots of wild boars where we live and those beastly animals seem to hide everywhere. I smell them sometimes near, sometimes far, but always there. I have taken it upon myself to chase after them a few times but whether with Bill or Chris or with both of them they never seem to let me wander off too far, I suppose they are protecting me too. Once I happened to get right on top of one of those ugly animal, sleeping under a tree in the woods. Well hearing me it took off like a shot with me in its trail. We went up the hill at full speed, the wild boar darting left and right, with me on its heels. But finally I lost him in some real thick part of the woods. Luckily for me, Bill and Chris always carry a whistle and when I go away from them for too long, they blow on it. I have learnt to recognize the sound and respond really well to that call. I was therefore able to join Chris back where she was waiting for me. I can tell you that I was panting like a demented animal, the chase behind the boar had taken its toll, but it was such fun even if I didn't catch it!

Another time, I was walking at my usual pace, half running half sniffing. Something strange caught my eyes, a sort of long stick curled up near a stone. Being of a very curious nature, I came a bit closer to investigate. Well that stick gave me the scare of my life, it suddenly jumped up in the air and I was so surprised I jumped with it. Bill was doubled in two with laughter. I had awakened a big snake out of its comfortable nap. I can tell you I am careful with these strange sticks nowadays.

On some walks we go by the river and this is definitely one of my favourite outings. The river we go to is set in woods, and it flows all the way to the sea. The water is wonderfully clear and in the summer really warm. I dive in it as though I have suddenly been transformed into a fish. Bill throws a ball very far and I swim as fast as I can to get it. Sometimes I have to swim against the current which is very strong but I am a good swimmer and not scared of the water. Always get that ball back and I could stay there all day if it was possible.

Sometimes in the summer Bill and Chris take a picnic and that is top of the bill as I invariably get a little treat from the picnic basket. I am allowed this "out of meal times" reward for my swimming abilities.

Then it's time to leave this wonderful place and the return journey is through woods where I can run some more, roll in the mud to dry off much to Chris' dismay. But luckily all this mud soon dries off and falls off and I am as good as new.

We also sometimes go to this magical place called the mountains, whether in the winter or the summer. Winter is great fun, diving and running in the snow but a bit cold on the paws. But the summer escapades are great. We sometimes set off for the whole day, backpack on Bill's back. I know then it's going to be a great day.

Again all these wild places to explore, cascades to play in, miles and miles of grass covered in flowers to run in. There are those funny little animals called marmots. I suppose you could compare them to some kind of rabbit without the long ears. They are even more fun to chase than a cat. Of course I don't mean them any harm but when they do that funny call on the side of the mountain, a kind of whistling noise to warn their friends of danger nearby, this is something I cannot resist. I am off full pelt towards the noise, but of course these clever little things dive in their holes and I get there looking stupid with nothing to catch. I have never learnt though and keep on doing it, I think for the fun of the chase.

Then of course last but not least there are the walks by the beach. That has to be the best. All that amazing and soft yellow stuff to run in, so good to feel under the paws. I could run for hours in it. The playing in the water where I catch my favourite ball, splashing away happily. At first I was a bit weary of the waves, not quite sure what to make of this surge of water coming at me, but I soon learnt that there was no harm in it and I can jump over it and swim away. The water tastes funny though and it's not too pleasant to get a mouthful of sand and water but this discomfort is worth it and easily forgotten for all the fun I am having.

I must admit that I am so grateful to my human pack Bill and Chris to give me all these opportunities to explore all of these wonderful places and give way to my naturally wild nature. After all this wilderness is always ready to surface back in any dog of any race but unfortunately through centuries of having to adapt to the humans way of life, whatever it may be, a great number of my fellow dogs have lost the wonderful "wild" in them. When I see one of those poor creatures being taken for a walk in the middle of nowhere but still tied up to a lead, I would love to be able to say to the owners "what a shame, why don't you teach your dog to respond to your orders, trust him and give it the chance to run free"! For myself, I know I am a better dog for being trusted and loved!

BILL

I read in one of the numerous books on dogs training a quote by one of the world's best known geniuses, Leonardo Da Vinci:

"Man has great power of speech, but the greater part thereof is empty and deceitful. The animals have little, but that little is useful and true; and better is a small and certain thing than a great falsehood"

This simple sentence is a good example of how the power of communication can be interpreted between humans and animals and in this particular case between humans and dogs.

In order to communicate with your dog you have to first understand and translate what your companion is trying to transmit to you. As the dog is not physically equipped to pronounce words, it is essential that you interpret its body language. The eyes, the stance, the mouth, its moods, all these can show signs of communication.

In our family, Chris seems to have the knack to understand most of Bella's signs of communication, whether is it stress, happiness, worry, fear, the tell tales are there, all so clear.

One other part of Bella behaviour is her ability to anticipate our movements. Do animals and dogs in particular have a power of prediction, now this would be a great mystery to resolve. It is known that in the wild, animals seem to sense danger well ahead of any danger perceived by humans, whether natural disasters such as fire or earthquake, but also can sense danger coming from other animals.

When Bella looks at me in the eye I think to myself "well Bella do you think what I am thinking ?" and I believe she responds in the same way : "do you think what I am thinking ?". Whether I have moved a certain way, or reached for something which may indicate a certain command, she seems to be totally aware of what is coming next. I know that a great number of people will laugh at this theory but it is my firm belief that animals comprehend our thoughts and feelings far better than we realise.

Bella has lived with us for nearly seven years and it seems that the teaching and training we have given her has stimulated her brain in such a way that she needs very little gesture from us to understand what we expect of her. For example, we were walking recently in the forest, Bella about one fifty metres in front of us. We came to a road where there was the possibility to carry straight on or turn left or right. I said to Chris, try to direct Bella to go left. Chris called Bella who looked back and immediately responded to Chris' hand command indicating left. And off Bella went, left turn. I presume that how shepherds communicate in the open with their faithful and clever sheepdogs.

However, Bella is definitely not trained to keep sheep. We used to live on a farm where the shepherd would bring his flock every year before the big walk to the mountain. Bella had befriended the big mountain sheepdog and used to go and say hello to him. However she went there one evening when the electrified wire has been switched on. On touching it she yelped like mad. This did not happen once but twice and since then I am sure she thinks that the sheep were responsible for her being hurt. She definitely does not like them and in fact when confronted with any of these animals, definitely turns her back on them seeming to say "I don't want to know you or have anything to do with you", the same attitude she had with her first obedience trainer who hurt her with one of the training strangling collar.

Getting back to the possibility of animals to have extrasensory powers, I wish some clever scientist would do some very serious research on the subject. Of course there may be a reaction to certain movements from the owner which the dog will interpret in its own way but I strongly believe that more than understanding a dog can anticipate. I have read lots of books on the subject and work has been done already. It seems that sometimes something happens, how does Bella know about that, she seems to be very aware of things without me telling her anything in particular. After all the experts studies concerning the intelligence of dogs, I firmly believe that we, humans, are definitely missing something regarding their ability to understand.

For example if we are going out we say "Bella, look after the house", she goes in a corner and looks at us with a mixture of reproach and sadness in her eyes. Of course she will do "her keeping the house job" very well, she does it at night when we are at home and barks at anything moving, but I believe that when we leave the house she does not like it, her human pack is not there and she cannot look after it properly.

Having started Agility training with Bella at one particular club, I changed club two years ago for one nearer to the house. I must admit that I should have done this sooner as the training that both Bella and I receive in this new place is so much more thorough. The improvement when we do competitions can vouch for this. Plus the fact that there is a very easy and friendly atmosphere in the club, all the people are nice and that must reflect on the dogs themselves.

In effect, I was asked recently to train to become an Obedience Trainer and I am really enjoying it. I do and have done in the past two years a great deal of reading from books written by so many different authorities on dogs training, whether scientists, dog trainers or shepherds themselves. I have found all those books so interesting but the peculiar thing is that so many pages talking about different topics actually relate to things that unknowingly at the time I did with Bella's training or continue to do.

I must admit I have come a long way on my human understanding of dogs. Years ago, to me a dog was a dog and that was that, nice to pat from time and have around but I had other priorities on my mind. Perhaps this is one of the sad results of the relationship between humans and animals, humans being so involved with their everyday priorities that they seem to miss sometimes the bigger issues. But since training with Bella, bringing her up to be a responsible creature and part of our family, I have suddenly become attuned to a different way of thinking. Bella is possibly an exceptional animal, all the better for me and my wife but when I look back at what we have achieved, Bella being such a good dog in every respect I feel very proud of our achievements.

What I wish to emphasise mostly is the importance of observing your dog. All the books which I read and which were given to me by my family since they discovered my new interest about animals, often repeat: "Observe your dog", "try and find out why your animal has done a particular thing and for what reason". Dogs are sensible creatures, well most of them anyway and the ones who are not have unfortunately acquired their unsociable habits through the fault of their owners. So whatever a dog does you must try to understand the reason.

When I do the training for the Obedience Classes, I work with a wonderful experienced man. I stay in the background and look carefully how he approaches each problem relating to each dog. Sometimes I do not agree with his analysis of a particular situation and we discuss this after the class. But through sheer observation, I am able to understand most of the behaviour of each dog and why that dog is acting a certain way.

There is of course so much more for me to learn, I am still in the infancy of that long study which is relationship between a human being and his dog. But the subject is infinitely interesting and I shall persevere to acquire new skills about it.

Finally I just want to quote a few sentences from a book written by John Pezzant, entitled "Shepherds and their dogs". To me these sentences resume all I believe in dog training.

In one paragraph, the writer says: "*The passer-by can ask himself what alchemy has taken place that the dog can be controlled at such distance and out of sight of his master. But there is no magic involved. This great feat is something far more fascinating and commendable: a partnership. On one side there is complete trust and on the other side, absolute devotion. And though not many shepherds would admit it, this is a relationship based on love".*

On another page, the writer says: *"When the dog is a pup, it is taught to obey a call at once. It must be done with kindness or the dog won't love you as he must if he is to serve you well"*

"Make a dog love you and he will never fail or forsake you".

"Work through gentleness, patience and firmness. I do not know one shepherd who handles his dogs with harsh severity, I would not care to know such a man".

"Be infinitely patient; do not offend your dog; do not easily be offended by him. Some dogs can bear much correction. Some are sensitive and can bear little. Study both. Avoid corporal punishment.

Perhaps I can talk about Bella as this writer does when he says about his high-spirited working Collie *"He clings to his freedom and will not do what he believes to be wrong, but his honest heart is still his master's, for whom he lives, breathes and fights.*

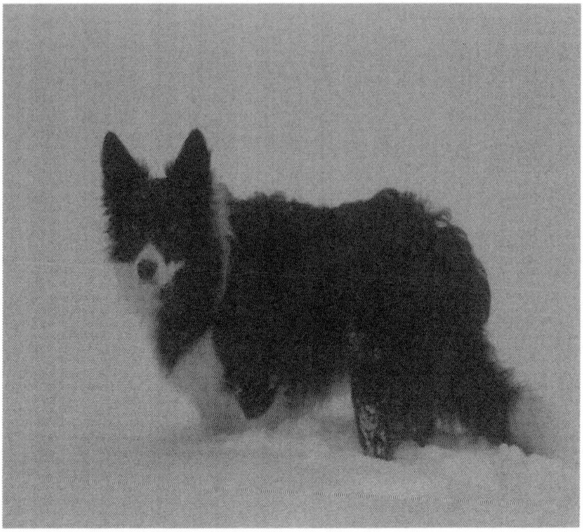

BELLA

My life is fun and full of surprises but sometimes I encounter events which can be frightening. I particularly think of the one time when I spent one week with my old folks, Samba and Chico and their human pack Lise and Sven. They used to live in a big house with a big garden not far from our home but they have now moved to the seaside in a small apartment with a tiny garden, too small for us three busy dogs to run to our usual full speeds.

Lise is very good and takes us out every day but when we leave the place we first have to be put on a lead which is a bit of a shame, but we don't mind, the three of us, mum, dad and daughter walking in our best educated manner, so well behaved that people's heads turn around in surprise to see such good dogs. We know that the tied up bit won't last and that afterwards we shall be FREE. Free to run together having such fun, exploring the woods with, for me, all these new and unknown smells as well as new encounters. Even met with other border collies that didn't belong to our family nor went to the same school as I do, but as all border collies are, so polite and sociable.

One day, when Sven went to play tennis, Lise decided to take us on a new walk on an unexplored area. This was all very exciting even for my parents who had never been there, and the three of us were having a ball of a time. But at this point tragedy struck. We had arrived in an old abandoned camping site, where humans like to congregate in the summer and supposedly have a rest and a holiday. The place was littered with electric wires which had been vandalised probably by silly human kids and it all looked very dangerous.

Being a good daughter, I was staying near my mum and we somehow got separated from Lise and my dad. We were totally lost and my mum, who is no longer a young chick, couldn't jump over those wires. We could hear Lise whistle and call but we could not find a way to get out. Of course I couldn't abandon my mum. I wouldn't have had any problem jumping over those wires but she couldn't.

We were desperately running around, looking for a way out, but to no avail, we were surrounded by those electric wires which so frightened my mum. My dad Chico had disappeared, probably listening to Lise's calls and trying to fetch her to come to us.

Finally my mum managed to get over her fears of the wires and searching frantically she found a way out of this labyrinth. I followed her, so relieved to be out of this dangerous place.

We found ourselves on a road and somehow my mum remembered the way to the flat. In no time we found ourselves in front of the gate where my parents human pack live. A very nice man who, I learnt later, is the keeper of these flats, opened the gate for us and took us to his apartment. We met with his dog, a lovely Labrador dog called Furious, but who didn't look scary at all.

After a while Lise arrived back, so worried but so happy to find us both alright. She had found my dad Chico in the woods looking for everybody, but as she explained to Sven later on, the fact that I had stayed with my mum reassured her as she knew that the two of us together would manage to find a way home.

Of course I found it quite normal to stay with my mum, when the old folks get older, the younger ones have to look after them.

This little adventure with my mum was finally great fun and I hope we can to it again!

Apart from that very daring pal down the road, "Gaston" who is actually a real good friend, never getting discouraged by my haughty behaviour towards him, I also have a few other good doggy friends. The very first one was "Smuts", a peasant really but such good fun. He used to live quite far away from our house but being a free spirit he would escape every morning from his house to do his little tour around the neighbourhood. Not much to look at, most of the time very dirty and in very good need of a bath, he would saunter in the morning in our garden to say hello. We would run around together, pretending to play fight, daring each other, and then he would leave to go on his daily walk. He had a very funny way of walking, having been hit by a car, he would have a kind of sideway walk. Sometimes, when we were on our walk with Chris, he would suddenly appear, and we would go off together, much to Chris's despair who would call me to come back. Smuts knew all the short cuts no humans could walk into and this would be such an adventure exploring all these new places with him. Sadly, I heard that he had become very ill and went away to wherever dogs go to after leaving this earth.

"Gaston" is another case of a faithful friend. In the morning, its mistress takes him for walks past our house. Inevitably, he wants to come and say hello and tries to play "macho" man with me. But he knows that he can only go that far and then he is quickly put back in its place by me. But his visit is something to look forward to every morning although I always pretend I am absolutely not interested.

One morning, I heard an unknown bark in the house next to ours, where no one lives. But surprise, some humans were there and with them appeared a dog which made me go weak at the knees. A wonderful creature, very majestic, a German shepherd, called Romeo. And he really deserved its name. Usually of a shy nature, I didn't hesitate and sauntered towards him to say hello. But after the usual social gestures which dogs use with each other, and to my total despair, he just walked off majestically, completely ignoring me. I was devastated and my ego really took a beating !

I also have a good many friends at the canine club where Bill and I go for training, but they are all so noisy, always barking, whimpering, until I can bare it no longer and just take refuge in the car. Such childish attitude from some of them, total spoilt brats.

One of my best friends is Ella Fitzgerald, my parents' cat. It's always great fun to meet her.

Here I am on the left with my mum and dad in my garden.

BILL

It seems that by some miracle, a dog can anticipate your intentions. For example, Bella will know when she is going to be taken out for a walk. However it is not a miracle, she has no divine powers to tell the future, she simply uses her ability to associate certain gestures we humans make to going for a walk, a habit formed message. Putting on certain clothes or shoes, mobile in the jacket pocket, tearing a piece of kitchen roll and placing it into coat pocket. But of course she goes absolutely mad when we go into the garage and unhook her collar and lead. She knows …….. it is "walkie" time. A dog's intelligence is such that they can deduct from certain habit forming gestures on their owners' part what is going to be the result of these gestures. And don't tell me that is not INTELLIGENCE!

Bella wakes up every morning (and us at the same time) about 6am. Even when the clocks change twice a year. Something seems to trigger it, same applies for the routine at night time, and she will be in front of her box of food dead at 5.30pm. It may be a call from her stomach of course but it is so regular that I firmly believe that there seems to be a clock ticking in her head. At night of course, she knows when it is time to go to sleep and curls up quite happily on her bed when we go to bed ourselves. She will however wait until we both go to bed, if one of us stays up later, she will wait and do her last minute check up outside with a good bark to let the enemy know that she is going to bed but they better stay away anyway !

Dogs do have memories. A dog will remember bad treatments, happy times, friendly dogs they have met, different places. One very famous Border collie in America can understand and remember nearly one thousand different words.

Commands:

Give your dog lots of loving and patience when trying to train it. You will also need to find the key factor which motivates your dog to obey. No motivation equals no successful training. No need to shout or pull your dog about. How would you react if someone was to pull you about, instinctively you would pull the other way, your dog has the same instinctive reaction.

Chewing things equals a game and a toy to a dog, they would have no more respect for your slipper than for a rubber toy. Right versus wrong, safe versus dangerous, self-interest equals no desire to please if not in the dog's interest. Opportunity – if food is within reach equals eat it now, the law of the jungle. But don't forget that your dog is a highly social creature, needs bonding whether with other dogs in the family or if the only pet needs bonding with its human pack. IT WILL NOT EASILY COPE WITH ISOLATION.

Once you have gone through this little book, I sincerely hope that you get a better understanding of your four-legged friend. My best advice for someone who acquires a puppy is to find a canine club nearby where your pet can meet other dogs, other people and trainers who can help both owner and dog. Do not be put out if things seem difficult at first, persevere and stay for a while until you feel your dog is happy with other dogs and other people but most of all, happy with you. Trainers in dog clubs will give you confidence how to handle any situation with your dog, they have the experience and as it is done on a voluntary basis, there is no financial reward for this job, just the satisfaction of teaching dogs. They are totally dedicated to this task.

One last thing I would like to add is that having read so many books about dogs' education and behaviour, most of them written by extremely professional people who have done a lot of research on the subjects, having read all these books, some several times, it is my firm belief that us humans are missing something about our understanding of dogs. I hope that one day, we do find this missing link, and then humans and dogs will have a much happier life together.

I must add that I could never have done this book without my wife Chris. We worked together to put all my ideas and strong convictions on paper and of course I couldn't have done it without Bella. I would never have thought in a million years that a dog could GIVE ME SO MUCH AND TEACH ME SO MUCH. We are still working together after seven years and it is so much fun even now, so THANK YOU BELLA FOR BEING BELLA!

I intend to write another book following this one, still about dogs, and it will be about the Adventures of Bella. This should be fun!

BELLA

I can't speak, I can't write, but I have no problem making myself be understood. Body language suffices, and that is common to all dogs. Unfortunately humans, who long ago, used to have the same ability to communicate, seem to have lost this ability to talk to one another by gestures or facial expressions. Now it's all talk, the louder the better it seems. We dogs do not need to be so noisy apart from when we bark and although the humans seem to think that most of the time we bark for nothing, this is such a misconceived idea. We make noise barking for a reason whether it would be warning, happiness, unhappiness, anger, fear. So please, look at us and try to read the signs we try to give you, relationships will become so much more wonderful between dogs and humans.

Please dog owners, do not leave your animal on its own all day. We are sociable creatures, we need to be part of a family. How do you think we feel when we hear the door closing on us and know that there will be no one around for hours? It is so sad. No wonder some of the more unruly dogs become nervous and get up to all sorts of mischief. Please think of us and see if a neighbour or even a dog walker can take us out during all these hours you are absent from the home. Although it would be walks on a lead, it would be better than all these long sad hours looking at the wall. Owners think that they are treating us kindly by leaving us inside, and to a certain extent this is true, but what about our feelings?

BILL

I cannot end this story without giving two special mentions.

First of all to Marise, who taught me all I know up to now about dog training, her invaluable and tireless help in improving both man and animal and without whom I would have never discovered this new passion in me – DISCOVERING THE MYSTERIES OF RELATIONSHIP BETWEEN DOG OWNERS AND THEIR EVER FAITHFUL ANIMALS.

A special thank you to the Club in Grasse where I became a member some years back, its atmosphere, its caring, its facilities and the devotion each member of the benevolent staff shows towards their club members and their four-legged companions.

8480580R00074

Printed in Great Britain
by Amazon.co.uk, Ltd.,
Marston Gate.